Amazing Animals

Anacondas

James De Medeiros

WEIGL PUBLISHERS INC.

Published by Weigl Publishers Inc.
350 5th Avenue, Suite 3304, PMB 6G
New York, NY 10118-0069

Amazing Animals series ©2009
WEIGL PUBLISHERS INC. www.weigl.com

Library of Congress Cataloging-in-
Publication Data

De Medeiros, James.
  Anacondas / James De Medeiros.
     p. cm. – (Amazing animals)
  Includes index.
  ISBN 978-1-59036-960-9 (hard cover :
alk. paper) – ISBN 978-1-59036-961-6
(soft cover ; alk. paper)
  1. Anaconda–Juvenile literature. I.
Title.
  QL666.063D46 2009
  597.96'7–dc22

2008003754

Editor
Heather Kissock
Design and Layout
Terry Paulhus, Kathryn Livingstone

Photograph Credits
Every reasonable effort has been made
to trace ownership and to obtain
permission to reprint copyright material.
The publishers would be pleased to have
any errors or omissions brought to their
attention so that they may be corrected
in subsequent printings.

Cover: Shutterstock; **Alamy:** pages 9,
10, 12, 18, 21; **Corbis:** page 19; **Getty
Images:** pages 1, 2, 3, 4, 5, 6, 7, 8,
11, 14, 15, 16, 17 bottom, 20, 23.

Printed in the United States of America
  2 3 4 5 6 7 8 9 0 12 11 10 09

About This Book

This book tells you all about
anacondas. Find out where they
live and what they eat. Discover
how you can help to protect them.
You can also read about them in
myths and legends from around
the world.

Words in **bold** are explained in the
Words to Know section at the back
of the book.

Useful Websites

Addresses in this book
take you to the home
pages of websites that
have information
about anacondas.

All of the Internet URLs given in
the book were valid at the time
of publication. However, due to
the dynamic nature of the Internet,
some addresses may have changed,
or sites may have ceased to exist
since publication. While the author
and publisher regret any
inconvenience this may cause
readers, no responsibility for any
such changes can be accepted by
either the author or the publisher.

Contents

4   Meet the Anaconda

6   A Very Special Animal

8   Senses

10 How Anacondas Eat

12 Where Anacondas Live

14 Enemies

16 Growing Up

18 Under Threat

20 Myths and Legends

22 Quiz

23 Find out More

24 Words to Know/Index

Meet the Anaconda

Anacondas are snakes that are very long and heavy. They live in South American swamps and rivers. The two most common anacondas are the green and the yellow.

These huge snakes are **reptiles**. This means they are cold-blooded. They depend on sunlight or warmth to stay alive. Their bodies must get enough warmth, or the snakes will die.

▼ Anacondas live alone and are rarely found in a group.

The Snake Family

- There are four different types of anacondas. They are the yellow, green, Bolivian, and the dark-spotted.

- Anacondas are closely related to boas and pythons. These snakes squeeze their **prey**.

▲ Like the anaconda, emerald tree boas live in South America.

A Very Special Animal

Anacondas have eyes on the top of their heads. This allows them to have almost all of their body in water and still see if anything is passing by.

An anaconda has very strong muscles throughout its body. These muscles help the anaconda move on land and in water. When moving from one place to another, the anaconda tightens and relaxes the muscles on either side of its body. This pushes the snake forward. Due to the wavy pattern the snake makes, the movement is often called **serpentine**.

▼ The green anaconda has black spots on its green back. Its body is olive-green or brownish in color.

Both yellow and green anacondas are covered with spots. The spots help **camouflage** the snake when it is in the grass.

The head of the anaconda is big and thick.

The anaconda's body is covered with scales. When moving on land, the snake uses its belly scales to grip the ground.

Anacondas have very sharp teeth. They curve backward to help the snake keep a firm grip on its prey.

An anaconda's jaws can open very wide. This allows the snake to swallow large animals.

Senses

Anacondas use their tongues to smell. When an anaconda sticks its tongue in the air, it is collecting smells. When the tongue goes back into the mouth, the smells are sent to the snake's brain, and the snake is able to tell if any animals are around. It can then track down its prey.

Anacondas also use their lips when hunting. Heat-sensing pits along their lips pick up the warmth of nearby animals. This helps the anaconda find animals that are within striking range.

▶ Anacondas have poor eyesight. The shape of their eyes makes it hard for them to see during daylight.

More about Senses

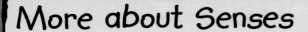

- Anacondas are very sensitive to vibrations from the ground. They can tell if an animal is moving closer to them from the weight of the vibration.

- When ready to mate, a female anaconda releases a unique smell. This guides male anacondas to her location.

How Anacondas Eat

Anacondas eat many types of animals. Birds, reptiles, fish, deer, and other **mammals** are all part of an anaconda's diet.

Anacondas are ambush hunters. They wait in the water until an animal gets close. They then lunge forward and grab the animal with their teeth. The anaconda coils its body around the other animal. As the animal struggles to escape, the anaconda squeezes tighter until its prey dies. Anacondas are called **constrictors** because of the way they kill their prey.

▼ The size of the animals eaten by anacondas can range from a small bird to a large alligator.

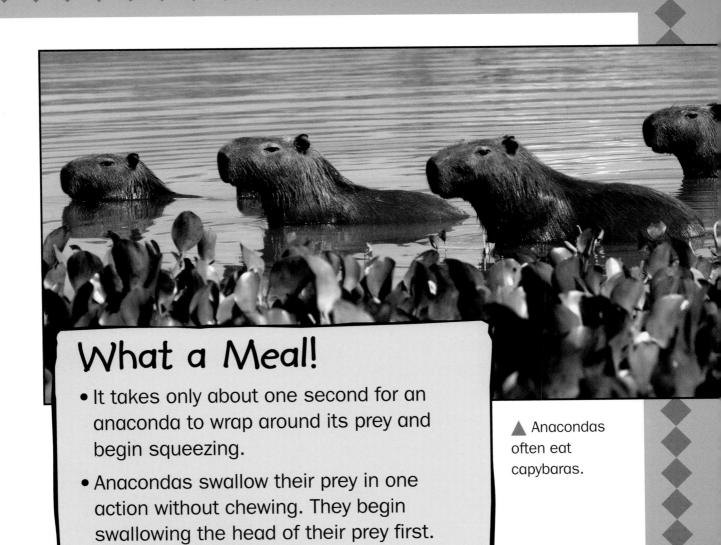

What a Meal!

- It takes only about one second for an anaconda to wrap around its prey and begin squeezing.

- Anacondas swallow their prey in one action without chewing. They begin swallowing the head of their prey first.

- Anacondas may go weeks without eating because they digest their food very slowly.

▲ Anacondas often eat capybaras.

Where Anacondas Live

Anacondas live in the **tropical** rain forests of South America. They can be found along the Amazon River in Brazil and in other wet areas, such as swamps and streams.

The size of an anaconda's **home range** depends on the seasons. South America has a rainy season and a dry season. During the rainy season, rivers and streams are overflowing with water. At this time, an anaconda can travel within a large area. When the dry season occurs, much of the water dries up. The anaconda cannot travel as far. It will stay in the small pools of water that remain.

▶ Anacondas live in water that moves slowly and is not very deep.

Anaconda Range

Trinidad and Tobago
Venezuela
Guyana
Suriname
French Guiana
Colombia
Ecuador
SOUTH AMERICA
Peru
Brazil
Bolivia
PACIFIC OCEAN
Paraguay
ATLANTIC OCEAN
Argentina
Uruguay

N
W E
S

0   500   1,000 km
0   311   622 mi

Green Anacondas
Yellow Anacondas
Yellow and Green Anacondas
No Anacondas

Enemies

Anacondas are the largest **predators** in South America. Most animals try to stay away from anacondas. Very few animals prey on them.

An anaconda is at its weakest when it has just eaten. The food forms a lump in its body, and the snake cannot move quickly. Large animals, including the jaguar, will attack an anaconda when it is in this condition. If an anaconda senses that danger is close-by, it moves back into the water. It only comes back out when it is safe.

▼ The jaguar is the third-largest type of cat in the world.

Useful Websites

www.nature.org

To learn more about anacondas, visit this website, and search "anaconda."

▲ Caimans are nocturnal animals. This means they are more active at night.

Living with Anacondas

There are many animals that live in the same areas as anacondas.

- caimans
- capybaras
- jaguars
- piranhas
- toucans
- wild pigs

Growing Up

It takes at least six months for a female anaconda to give birth to a litter. A litter of anacondas contains between 20 and 100 babies. Anaconda babies are born live and can swim, hunt, and care for themselves shortly after birth.

A green anaconda baby is about 2 feet (61 centimeters) long at birth. It continues to grow throughout its life. As the anaconda becomes bigger, it outgrows its skin. When this happens, new skin grows, and the snake sheds its old skin. Baby anacondas shed their skin for the first time when they are about one week old.

▼ Young anacondas fall prey to animals such as the ocelot, a member of the cat family.

Growth Chart

Newborn anacondas are 1 to 3 feet (0.3 to 0.9 meters) long.

Green anacondas grow to be about 16 feet (5 m) long.

Some anacondas reach lengths of 26 feet (8 m).

▼ Scientists must be very careful when measuring an anaconda, or they may get hurt.

Under Threat

Humans are the main threat to the anaconda's survival. Anacondas are killed so their skin can be used for clothing. Humans have often killed the snakes because they are afraid of them.

▼ The selling of anaconda skin has caused the number of snakes to decrease in some parts of South America.

People are destroying the anaconda's **habitat**. They put buildings and roads in areas where the snakes live. This drives the anaconda's prey out of the area. Without food to eat and a place to live, the anaconda cannot survive.

Useful Websites

www.wcs.org

Visit this website to learn about how people are trying to help save the anaconda and many other animals.

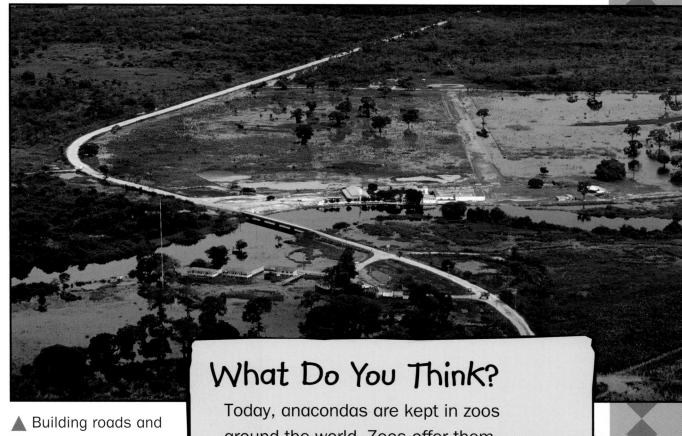

▲ Building roads and towns harms the anaconda's habitat. As the habitat changes, so does the life of the anaconda.

What Do You Think?

Today, anacondas are kept in zoos around the world. Zoos offer them a safe environment, but there is far less space for them to move around. Should zoos keep anacondas in captivity? Should anacondas be in their natural habitats?

Myths and Legends

The anaconda plays an important role in the lives of South America's Aboriginal Peoples. Some believe that their **ancestors** were anacondas. The snakes became human when they first shed their skin.

To some Aboriginal groups, the anaconda plays the role of protector. One group believes that its people are protected by the eagle, the jaguar, and the anaconda. The group believes that each animal guards one part of their world.

▶ Some Aboriginal Peoples believe the anaconda protects the rivers. The jaguar is believed to watch over the land, and the eagle looks after the sky.

A folktale from another Aboriginal group refers to a mountain that is guarded by a large eagle and an anaconda. When people began to light campfires near the mountain, they angered these guardians. The eagle and the anaconda made a rainstorm to stop the campfires from burning.

▶ The anaconda plays an important role in many South American festivals.

Quiz

1. Where do anacondas live?
(*a*) **deserts** (*b*) **farms** (*c*) **swamps**

2. How many different kinds of anaconda are there?
(*a*) **two** (*b*) **four** (*c*) **six**

3. What body part do anacondas use to smell?
(*a*) **tongue** (*b*) **eyes** (*c*) **jaw**

4. When does a baby anaconda begin to shed its skin?
(*a*) **after one day** (*b*) **after one week**
(*c*) **after one year**

5. What do anacondas eat?
(*a*) **vegetables** (*b*) **plants** (*c*) **animals**

Answers: 1. (c) Anacondas live in swamps.
2. (b) There are four kinds of anaconda.
3. (a) Anacondas smell with their tongue.
4. (b) Anacondas begin to shed their skin after one week.
5. (c) Anacondas eat animals.

Find out More

To find out more about anacondas, visit the websites in this book. You can also write to these organizations.

National Audubon Society
700 Broadway
New York, NY 10003

The Nature Conservancy
4245 North Fairfax Drive, Suite 100
Arlington, VA 22203-1606

World Wildlife Fund
United States
1250 24th Street NW
Washington, DC 20037

Words to Know

ancestors
people from the past
camouflage
blending in with one's environment
constrictors
animals that squeeze other animals
to death
habitat
the natural area where animals live
home range
the area in which an individual
animal lives

mammals
animals with either hair or fur that care
for their young by feeding them milk
predators
animals that hunt other animals for food
prey
an animal that is hunted for food
reptiles
cold-blooded animals, such as lizards,
crocodiles, turtles, and snakes
serpentine
winding or twisting
tropical
very hot and humid

Index

Aboriginal Peoples 20

green anaconda 4, 5, 6, 7, 13, 16, 17

litter 16

prey 7, 8, 10, 11, 16, 18

skin 16, 18, 20, 22
smell 8, 9, 22
South America 4, 5, 12, 13, 14, 18, 20
swamps 4, 12, 22

teeth 7, 10

yellow anaconda 4, 5, 7, 11, 13